SLOW RIVERS
Poems From My Sixties

Joseph Neely

Cover art: Janice Warner
ISBN: 979-8-218-43822-7
Library of Congress Control Number: 2024913629
Printed in the USA
First Edition

Slow Rivers Press
Ann Arbor, Michigan, USA
slowriverspress.com

For Madison and Murphy:
loved by many, gone too soon.

Always and especially for Linda.

I told my wife a lot of recovering alcoholics drink coffee all day or smoke like fiends. And some write poems, she observed. Some write poems.

WARM-UP EXERCISES

*Meatless Mondays sound great
on Tuesday or Wednesday,
though come Sunday evening
the idea has lost some charm.*

*I have foreseen my death in a dream.
I'm driving behind an older woman—
sometimes it's an older man—
who stops for no reason
before entering a traffic circle.
The only consolation is that she dies, too.*

A FEW HAIKU

*no energy like
street full of happy children
first warm day of spring*

*rain and wind blow in
titmouse and a cardinal
still sing in the storm*

*grandchildren frolic
in big Lake Michigan waves
the torch has been passed*

*winter morning walk
woodpeckers' bright rhapsody
tat-tat-tat-tat-tat*

Preface

I wrote the first of these poems to preserve the moment a granddaughter announced she ran faster than a cheetah. I was pleased with that poem and wrote more. All the poems in this book were written when I was in my mid-to-late 60s.

I have applied varying degrees of diligence to writing poetry since junior high school, but publishing my work was never a priority until I began to consider my legacy. What could I leave behind so that an undreamed-of descendant might come to know me, many years after I'm gone? Had I waited too long? Would anyone care?

I did not need to look far to find an example of late-life renewal and achievement. Dave Miller and I grew up in the same neighborhood and have been friends since we were twelve years old. A few years ago, largely retired and in his mid-60s, Dave whipped himself into shape and trekked through the Andes Mountains to Machu Picchu in Peru. Two years later Dave hiked to the summit of Mt. Elbert, the highest point in the Rocky Mountains.

James Lee Burke, one of America's great writers, believes a novel published when he was in his mid-80s to be his best work. Think about that. With short story collections and novels dating back more than 60 years, and after winning numerous prizes and awards including a Guggenheim Fellowship, James Lee Burke is doing his best work as he closes in on 90. Like James Lee Burke, I consider my most recent work to be my best. There is a sense of acceptance and vulnerability in these poems which was absent from my earlier work.

I am fortunate; not everyone is able to pursue late-life passions. I lost a beloved brother-in-law to dementia when he was in his 60s, and the list of deceased classmates at my 50th high school reunion was depressingly long.

What's still on your list?

The Poems

A PLAYGROUND GIFT

"I run fast as a cheetah!"
you told me on the playground
and in proof wobbled across
a wooden-slat bridge,
faster than the spotted cat
in your picture book at home.
"So fast I can't even see you!"
I exclaimed, and in wondrous joy
you crossed the span again.

Passersby saw an old man
and a happy little girl
playing in the morning sun.
But you were on the Serengeti
and, for just a moment, so was I.

LEAVING VICTORY PARK
Cleveland, 1967

We left the pool together
after such fun with friends
that you risked being late
and my bike's banana seat
made easy what was awkward
so you climbed aboard
and I pedaled slowly,
willing the journey to last.
You had no choice,
I know that now.

"We'll never get there in time,"
you said, and I was embarrassed
but knew you understood
by the trusting way
you held on to my hips
when I stood on the pedals
and churned furiously
towards your home.

We arrived as your family
gathered at the table
and you would pay no penalty
for my romantic dawdling.
I set off for my own home
and my own family meal.

That was my introduction
to the true nature of love,
the moment I understood
love was more complicated
than a pretty girl,
a Schwinn Stingray
and a bright summer day.

WE WERE BUT TWELVE

What would she think,
this girl I once knew,
to learn that even now
she flits through my dreams?

We are still twelve in the night,
our palms as sweaty and love as pure
as on that day we held hands
for a few racing beats of our hearts.

Oh sweet dreams of childhood,
brief visions of wonder and joy.
Oh sad dreams of innocence,
never again to be that boy.

EUGENE'S PLAYBOYS

Eugene promised to leave his Playboys
when his family moved away,
and having been almost invited
my brother and the neighborhood boys
boosted me through the milk chute
on the side of Eugene's house,
and I opened the door
so everyone could tiptoe in.

Quickly overwhelmed by our crime—
nice boys don't break into homes
in search of naked ladies—
we looked around half-heartedly
though no one dared
descend the basement stairs,
where we agreed it most likely
Eugene had stashed his cache.

Suddenly something spooked us,
and we ran outside as if
the Devil himself were chasing us,
and, indeed, perhaps he was.

So it's possible those naked ladies
are moldering away on top of the ductwork
in the darkest part of that basement
on Belvoir Boulevard in Cleveland,
but I'm almost certain now
that Eugene's Playboys
were never there at all.

[I loved Rod McKuen's poems]

I loved Rod McKuen's poems
in Mr. McMullen's English class,
where he wore rumpled wool
and carried a fragrant pipe
deep in his suitcoat pocket.

Later I learned those poems
were disdained by the acclaimed
but nothing moved me like that
when I was thirteen,
responding only to emotion
in poetry and in life.

My father's suits were crisp
and he shined his best shoes
Sunday nights at the kitchen table
before flying off to sell furnaces
in Fort Wayne or Frontenac.
My father tried a pipe once
but went back to Camel straights,
which he allowed me to steal
while pretending not to notice.

I miss my father and Mr. McMullen
and the days when simple poems
gave voice to things I couldn't name
and sometimes made me cry
when no one was watching.

THE JERSEY

I know what that means,
my father growled,
and I too ashamed
to admit I did not.

I was twelve and understood only
that the number on my jersey
was somehow sexual,
with almost no concept
of what that might mean.

I slunk away before my father
could grab me by that jersey
and put an end to my foolishness,
as fathers often did in 1967
when the world was still young.

I wore it for an afternoon, showing off
for friends no smarter than I,
then left that jersey in the dunes,
relieved of rebellion's responsibilities
and determined to reclaim my childhood
for the last few weeks of summer.

FULL CIRCLE

My son was twelve
when we last held hands,
walking through a parking lot
to buy bagels after church.

I sensed a car and reached out
to be sure he was safe
and he held on briefly but let go,
making clear he was suddenly
too old for holding hands.

And now we approach the day
when he'll take my hand
as we cross busy roads,
and I will try not to pull away,
for a father must never grow
too old for holding hands.

DISPLAYING SCHOOL PHOTOS

I have my own school photo this year
and will send a headshot
to all our children and stepchildren,
just as they send us, my wife and me,
school photos of grandchildren
every year in the fall.

Some grandparents create shrines,
but I have my own method
of displaying school photos.
I like to put them in a drawer
where they lie forgotten for years
until the day I find them—
usually while searching
for reading glasses or keys—
and so begins a journey
through years of pigtails and braces,
a tight-throated, stinging-eyed journey
through gains and losses now past,
each memory perfectly framed
in wallet-sized innocence.

Joseph Neely

HIGH SCHOOL HEROES
Maurice Reese, 1953 – 2020

My wife remembers the boys
chanting his name at school
Reese! Reese!
and I tell her of the time Maurice,
carrying a 12-pound shotput,
ran faster than a big man
had any right to run,
clay cinders flying
like sparks from his spikes,
passing runner after runner
at the Waterford Mott Relays
near Pontiac in 1971,
and how the astonished gasps
of every boy watching
mingled and rose
to fill the night sky.

[If family were defined by blood]

If family were defined by blood,
little ones would not cry out
to hold your hand and not mine
each time we cross a road,
and others would not run to me,
delighted and excited,
each time I stop by.

THE PERFECT AGE

He likes nothing quite so much
as when I propose "chicken?" or "zebra?"
each time he holds up a plastic cow.

Oh how he laughs
to think his grandfather
might really be so silly.

Oh what fun to be
ever-so-much-smarter
than this funny old man.

A GRANDDAUGHTER'S RUNES

This one will be a scientist
or perhaps a poet, filling a journal
with precisely rendered symbols
from a language she invented
in which she alone is fluent

for she has stories to tell
and truth to proclaim,
and will not wait
on anything so ordinary
as learning to write
when she has her own runes.

A GRANDDAUGHTER AT SIX

I am not surprised
you prefer the barn cat's
ragged ears and golden eyes
to the prancing high-bred filly
you were expected to love.

You set a table on the patio floor,
an invitation to little white dogs
paper napkins your Irish lace,
picnic plates and cups
placed elegantly on the planks.

Clapping, you bid them come.
and they respond eagerly,
drawn to this source of light,
this gentle force so different
from any other here today.

Bold and curious,
you share joy with a smile
and charm grown-up strangers
with frank and honest answers
when they expect little girl giggles.

I will remember this day
and pray that you remember, too,
this girl not yet learned
to fear or blend in, this girl
determined to share her heart.

YOUR MOST LOVED

Decorated with hearts and flowers,
your note proclaimed you loved me
to the moon and back
and assured me I was very VERY nice
but your love was also conditional.
I was to show your note to no one.
Not to Nana or your cousins. No one.

And, Dear One, I did not,
for I knew that one day
you would love someone else
as much as you loved me then,
and I was determined to remain
your most loved
for as long as I could.

GOD BLESS THE CHILD
a shy granddaughter's first day at school

May she find a friend today—
may every lonely child find a friend—
and may the adults who surround her
remember that for those who feel deeply
minor setbacks are felt as body blows

and when she finds a friend
and they chase across the playground
with no fear of stumbling,
please guide her to a soft spot
before she trips and falls.

THE 7:25

We call it the 7:25,
the Amtrak train
outbound for Chicago
shrieking its warning
each weekday morning
at the crossing nearby.

I first noticed the 7:25
while a grandson got ready for school,
he in kindergarten but already
handling challenges with aplomb,
and to this day I think of him
at every whistling train.

The 7:25 was late today, I tell him,
and he indulges me with a smile every time.

REMEMBER KING HENRY

The mistakes of youth
will one day make you cringe
but remember King Henry

for the entire kingdom was certain
he would always be Prince Hal,
an insubstantial boy

making merry with drunkards
and worth no more
than a box of tennis balls

but the Warrior King
won the day at Agincourt,
and wooed the princess for his bride.

So remember King Henry,
who began life the fool
but grew into his rule.

*And we understand him well
How he comes o'er us with our wilder days
Not measuring what use we made of them.
(Shakespeare, Henry V, Act 1, Scene 2)*

A POEM FOR YOU

When you were seven
I wrote a poem for you.
You jumped up and down,
thrilled to be my muse.

When you were twelve
I wrote a poem for you.
You hugged me and I sighed,
knowing what would come.

When you were seventeen
I wrote a poem for you.
You rolled your eyes,
thinking I would not see.

When your children were born
I wrote a poem for you
though you had no time to read,
your very life a poem.

When your children left home
you found the first poem I wrote
and wept. I sent a soft breeze
to remind you I'm still here.

A CHRISTMAS SONNET

Viewing a photo in which
he sits with a grandson
looking over a book filled
with colorful exotic animals,
the grandfather's first thought
is that he must lose weight

but the little boy is smiling,
delighted to have spotted
the Peruvian anteater
before his grandfather could
and not at all concerned
with double chins or waistlines.

Let us be gentle with ourselves at Christmas,
remembering only that which truly matters.

PRIORITIES

I did plan to re-join
you and the other adults
left behind at the Christmas table,
but find myself caught
between two granddaughters,
one with her head on my shoulder
and the other explaining a children's movie
in great and unnecessary detail,
while their brother stands near my feet
roaring like the Tyrannosaurus rex
we gave him when we arrived.

So, please, offer my apologies
and fill me in later
on what I need to know.

THE DAFFODIL FAIRIES

Fairies braided the daffodils
in front of the porch last night.
I can't wait to show the grandkids;
won't they think it grand?

I braided the leaves, my wife said,
so your friend Paul
won't chop down my daffodils
the way he chops down
everything else around here.
He's a madman with that weed whacker,
doesn't know a daffodil from a dandelion.

Fairies, I implore her. Please.
They won't believe us forever, you know.

Fine, she relented,
tell them it was fairies.
Just make sure your friend
stays away from my daffodils.

Joseph Neely

ON TAKING MY MOTHER AND STEP-FATHER TO A RESTAURANT IN SEATTLE

Perhaps the old Marine,
who seldom seems to follow
our conversation this night,
is not lost at all.

Perhaps he is thinking
of islands once stormed
and speaking with friends
who did not return.

His wife is more focused but envies
a vibrant younger woman nearby,
certain they would have been friends
in a different world and another time,

but the old warrior's wife is tired, too,
for it takes a courage different than his—
but courage nonetheless—
to care for this Marine she loves.

Bill McNabb, 1925 – 2015, USMC, South Pacific, WWII
Catherine Verschoor Neely McNabb, 1925 – 2018, Home Front

SHINY DIMES AND CARDINALS

My mother—
before her final years
of lunches with dead husbands
and visits with a granddaughter
who was not there—
promised she would try
to let us know what lay beyond
and she did try, after she died.

I found shiny dimes in odd places
and two bright red cardinals—
the husbands she loved
without the unworthy third—
pursued her across my lawn
that entire first spring,
flattering her immensely in the chase.

But she grew weary of parlor tricks,
or joined a book group and made friends,
for the dimes have disappeared
and the cardinals I see now
are not as bright or amorous
as the birds I saw then.

But I am not abandoned.
My mother still visits when I write,
suggesting an idea here
or a few words there,
to let me know she's fine.

Joseph Neely

ELEGY FOR A FRIEND
BJW, 1957 - 2021

A storm blew across the lake
two days after you died.
Lightning made visible the wind
and the waves attacking the shore.
Dawn's soft first light implied
a return to summer's glory,
but we are older now and wise.

We will learn to laugh again,
to cherish the memories
and gifts you left behind.
That was your wish
and we honor that request,
your very life a gift
though your time here too brief.

[Let us grow old together]

Let us grow old together.
I'll carry a pocketknife,
and drive so you can knit.
We'll run endless errands
and come home to nap
in our matching chairs.
We'll watch deer in the yard at dusk,
and in the morning take turns
banging on the window
to scare away the starlings.

THE NATURE OF LOVE

Today you asked
for a bite of my breakfast sausage
and I gave you all that I had left—
at least two-thirds—
insisting I really didn't want it
and had almost decided
not to cook sausage at all,
sausage to complete my breakfast
of steel cut oats and fruit.

I was happy when you popped
that beautifully-browned, perfectly-spiced
breakfast sausage into your mouth
with no idea of my sacrifice,
for such is the nature of love.

APOLOGIES

Apologies in love are difficult,
for it is not enough to regret
that feelings are hurt
or the one you love is angry.

No, you must confess your sins
and be truly sorry for the damage done
by your own undeniable stupidity.
It's hard; trust me, I know.

You could try buying flowers
and making a copy of this poem,
but forgiveness is never guaranteed
with even the most abject apology.

Joseph Neely

THE DEFINITION OF INSANITY

Clear proof of insanity
is eating tacos in the car,
after a late shift at Lowe's,
and believing that somehow
I will not arrive home
with lettuce, meat and cheese
decorating my belly mantle
and littering my lap.

Further proof is knowing
I will try again soon—
next week or next month—
convinced that this time
I'll arrive at my destination
clean-shirted and content.

WOOL SUITS AND BLUE JEANS

I have lived many lives,
worn wool suits with wingtips
or blue jeans with boots,
my hands sometimes calloused
though more often smooth,
and it took many years
to understand I was meant
to carry coffee in a thermos
and write poems when I could
at the picnic table in back
out behind the loading dock.

[When old men follow rivers]

When old men follow rivers
they are sometimes
dashed against dams
or swallowed by the Leviathan
alone and far from home

but I rise joyfully in the dark,
careful not to disturb
the old dog on your side
or his sister on mine
and do not fear weirs or whales

for your breath beckons the dawn
and I set forth to battle demons
I must face on my own,
assured of your forgiveness
when at last I come home.

THE CASCO BAY MAILBOAT

I knew my wife would make friends
with the old woman on the mailboat
which moves travelers and tourists
among the islands of Casco Bay.

She sat where we wanted to sit,
near the rail and out of the wind,
scowling to discourage conversation
with those she would never see again
before surrendering to my wife
and our small white dog.

We sat with her enthralled
by stories of eighty years
on Chebeague and other islands,
stories of isolation and heartbreak
but also pride and perseverance,
a life hard for us to imagine,
accustomed as we are to the safety
of our sheltered inland home.

A few days later we crossed
the Boothbay Harbor footbridge
and were greeted at a restaurant
by a woman from Ukraine
who cried when my wife
gave her a sunflower brooch
a few months after the cruel invasion
of her wheat and sunflower home.

ACCOMMODATIONS

Tonight is mish-mosh tea night,
tea made from already-spent bags
mixing flavors and brands
without regard to anything
except squeezing one more cup
from bags that most would toss
after the first use.

The tea is not good—
it's too thin or a discordant mixture
of flavors that should never be joined—
but my wife likes to stretch a dollar
and mish-mosh tea is a small price to pay
for maintaining marital bliss.

LOVE YOU, BRO

Love you, bro is a phrase
disguised as an after-thought
and spoken when leaving a room
so deniability is maintained
and we are held accountable
by our own choice alone.

But though I never asked,
you helped with my socks
when my knee wouldn't bend
and I couldn't dress myself
at the end of that August day
on a boat with our friends.

Thank you, bro.
Love you, too.

SIRIUS LOVE

Friends and old lovers lurk
along seldom-trod pathways
until we have trouble recalling
faces and voices we were certain
would remain clear forever.

Best to think of them kindly,
when we think of them at all,
to acknowledge them as memories
neither immensely cherished
nor profoundly grieved

and to hold close those few
warm and constant loves—
our night sky, North Star loves—
undemanding and undimmed
by the passage of time.

GREY FEBRUARY

After ten grey days
and with a storm on its way
two white swans
create the illusion
they are twice their size,
casting reflections
over the flat grey water
of a modest pond
in dull midday light
beneath a sullen sky.

But in this grey season
we seek comfort
wherever it might be found,
and pronounce it beautiful.

COLD AND LONELY MARCH

March is a fickle lover
intent on leaving
but not yet sharing her plans

for in the midst of a rare embrace
she looks over her shoulder
to plan her escape

and we barely dare dream of April
though on St. Patrick's Day we plant
lettuce, radishes and peas

an act of defiance and faith,
proof we have not surrendered
to cold and lonely March.

STACKING FIREWOOD

Summer evenings stretch out
with all the time we need
for trimming and planting,
and summer evenings allow
for less vital projects, too,
conceived and begun only
because there is time to dream
in warm unhurried summer.

But comes a night in August
when the sky darkens early
and we hurry inside to search
for a sweater last seen in April
and the only projects that matter
prepare us for the coming storm.

NOVEMBER WALK

geese rise in formation
from the river across the road

brown rust and ochre
now replacing red and yellow

and we are largely content
though acutely aware

it is not easy to keep
the dark lady at bay

through grey days and cold nights
of another long winter

so we pray some combination
of god love family memory

will keep us safe until
the trees turn green again

PALE LIGHT

November's morning sun
seems unsure whether to stay
before decreeing okay,
but no more than this.

Help us, Lord, for such pale light
is sometimes not enough
to keep us trudging forward
and into winter's maw.

WE MARK OUR LIVES

       The December field is deserted
     cornstalks lean drunkenly
   abandoned to the cold
alone in the lonely.
In November noisy
    raucous cranes were here
      feasting on the harvest's spillage
        as their inevitable journey drew near.

       In springtime the cranes will return
     a pair circling the sodden field
   sounding a dinosaur call
to claim their spot.
By Mother's Day
    eggs will hatch and
      colts will be cared for carefully
        until the next noisy departure.

PANDEMIC WINTER SUNRISE

We turn to the bird feeder
to avoid the morning news.
Juncos not flown south,
finches and chickadees
appear with the sun.
Next the black squirrel,
often bullied and chased
by larger grey cousins.

Today we allow him
to eat seeds fallen to the patio
and drink from the birdbath,
but pound on the window
when it becomes clear
he lusts after mealworms,
a treasure reserved
for bluebirds alone.

He darts off but will return,
knowing our vigilance wanes
and our tolerance varies greatly
from one day to the next.

THE SPARROW'S QUEST

Some sort of sparrow
somehow got inside,
perching and chirping
on the window sash
above the kitchen sink.

She was asking, we decided,
for fresh water in the birdbath,
March puddles still frozen
or on warm days too muddy
for a bird's proper bath.

We opened the window
and she quickly flew off,
greeted by worried wrens
and other anxious friends,
forever now their hero.

BORN A THIEF

With no reason for fear
the jay is still the nervous thief
jimmying an unwatched door
as if the chickadees might
join forces with the finches
to rush in and haul him away.

He grabs a peanut,
his from the start,
and darts off
proclaiming his birthright
from a nearby spruce.

Never trust a blue jay,
he shrieks with delight.
Never trust me or mine!

Joseph Neely

FRENZY AT THE FEEDER

they should all be gone by now
bedded down in nearby trees
but tomorrow they may not eat
so finches and sparrows
cardinals and chickadees—
even dark-eyed juncos
usually content with the spillage—
fight for footing on a peg
with the light nearly gone
and a February storm blowing in
where winter still reigns
and spring is but a rumor

THE ABSURDITY OF DREAMS

1.
The worst dreams are not those
where you are chased by monsters,
or stand in line naked
waiting for a train.

The worst dreams
make long-buried betrayal fresh,
and allow it to fester.

2.
I recall every frightening detail
of a dream in which I'm lost
and the man selling corn from a truck—
I know him from somewhere—
won't drive me or even point me home
though he clearly knows the way
and it's not far from here,
not far at all.

But the sun rises on a new day
and dream fogs begin to clear away,
the sky a robin egg's blue
for just a beat or two,
though I still hate that schmuck
selling corn from his truck.

3.
One of my wife's boyfriends from high school
joined us at a restaurant in Northern Michigan,
though as far as I could tell he was not invited
and the pandemic was in full swing,
the restaurant overwhelmed and understaffed.

He looked younger than I knew him to be,
the big dopey smile on his face
stretching out a foolish Fu Manchu,
a flowered nylon shirt with huge collars
unbuttoned deep down into his hairy chest.

My wife was delighted to see him
and put her arms around him from behind,
laying her head on his back
as if they were in the field at Woodstock
listening to Crosby Stills Nash & Young.

After way too long I cleared my throat
and my wife, roused from her reverie,
said, "Oh, Phil, this is my husband."
He shook my hand and called me Jeff,
so I called him Bruce for the rest of the night.

Mercifully, I awoke.

THE BARBERSHOP POEMS

1.
BEFORE HAIRSTYLISTS FOR MEN

Men were happier before hairstylists,
when barbers knew the score
of last night's game and who pitched,
trimmed eyebrows without asking
and could cut a Princeton
with one hand behind their back.

In those simpler times
men were certain their barbers
voted and rooted as they did,
though barbers seldom said more,
in response to barber shop blather,
than "Really? Well I'll be darned."

2.
SEARCHING FOR A TRIBE

My father's community of men
gathered at the Glo in Grand Haven—
where Ron called him Beautiful Carl
though my father's name was Ralph—
and at Spoto's in Cleveland,
where Vince spit-shined shoes
at his father's shop on Saturday.

I once had a barbershop, too
but ignorance replaced civility
and I now collect coupons
for cheap chain haircuts
from cashiers with scissors,
the names on their tags forgotten
the moment I leave

and I am often reminded—
by bristles growing from my ears—
how I miss that community of men.

TWO OLD DOGS

1.
The old shih tzu comes alert,
sensing the spirits of this house,
hearing voices and footsteps
we cannot hear.
We scratch behind his ears
urging him back to sleep
but he tumbles from the bed,
long past days of jumping
up or down without our help.

Unhurt and unafraid,
he begins a restless hunt
along the length of the hallway—
nails clicking on wood floors—
searching for the voice
he hears calling him
from a door slightly ajar
and behind which we hope
he will be waiting for us
when our own hunt is done.

2.
The beloved white terrier
sleeps peacefully a few feet
from chipmunks gathering acorns,
clearly visible outside on the porch.

She still sometimes pretends
she wants to chase them away,
but today she dreams of terrorizing
the entire chipmunk nation,
rather than concerning herself
with these few outside the door.

THE FARMER'S YARD

A gentle Michigan wind
dances over the farmer's yard,
giving me pause as I climb
high up into my Chevy truck
and balance this week's bounty—
beets, bacon, a bunch of kale—
on the passenger seat.

Soon my ears will sting,
my breath announce
the season's change,
but today barnyard birds
proclaim summer's plenty
and I would live nowhere
but among these peninsulas.

LOPEZ TACO HOUSE
Albion, Michigan

A sombrero still hangs over the door
and black velvet señoritas
in colorful peasant blouses
still smile coyly from the walls.

I confess that forty-five years ago
I came here many nights
after last call next door
at The Rusty Hinge.

"I don't drink anymore," I added,
an unprompted apology for chaos
sown long before my server was born.

"I've been saved, too," she said.

"I'm not saved, just sober."

She looked confused, then smiled.
"Yeah, sober," she said. "Same thing."

OCTOBER 10

In small-town Michigan
we watch woolly caterpillars
and note when cranes gather early
in the brown-stalk cornfields,
but a more reliable predictor
of the coming season's fury
is the date we first break out
our Carhartt coats.

Versace, I suppose,
in East Grand Rapids
or Grosse Pointe,
though I'm not really sure
about Saginaw or Flint.

NORTH SHORE DRIVE
Grand Haven, Michigan

Years beyond our childhood,
with every inch of shoreline
filled by arrogant mansions
built to the very edge of lots
intended for modest cottages,
you can still be alone on the beach
and let your dog run free
at seven-thirty in the morning.

THIS WIND

With no minnows for feasting
in the choppy waves below
the gulls hover and shriek,
rehashing the small victories
and lost chances of their lives,
on a blustering day in March
before the arrival of spring
along Lake Michigan's shore.

When the sun sets they form
a loose huddle on the beach
while this wind buries them in sand,
but they survive as we all survive
tucking their heads beneath a wing
and dreaming of better days.

OCCASIONALLY IN JUNE
northern Lake Michigan

Rising to grey skies,
with winds born on the Plains
blowing across the Big Lake,
it's hard to credit June today.

Coyotes stroll the beach
as if it were winter
and nearby homes abandoned,
while only newly budded trees
give lie to the certainty of snow.

But I have nowhere to go
and no one to please,
so I have no objection
to a wintry day in June—
no objection at all.

A VILLAGE IN MICHIGAN

A sign at the edge of town reads
'Home of the 1989 Cherry Festival Queen'
twenty-five years after her reign.
I'll pass through a dozen villages
on my peddler's rounds this day.

I wonder if she's still here,
her court now consisting of regulars
at the American Legion's fish fry,
where they profess their pride
but share her secret shame.
For all her gifts, she never left this place.
They would leave, of course they would,
if they only had the chance.

I cheer myself by deciding
she founded a home for children
somewhere with a lot of orphans,
and made love with rock stars
before breaking their hearts.

Warming to the task,
I'm certain she sips
champagne with royalty
and brings beautiful children
here each summer,
happy that friends no longer fear
her somewhere-else beauty.

I murmur a quiet prayer
that time has not stood still for her
as it has for her hometown,
as it sometimes has for me.
Just let her be happy, I pray,
driving towards the next village
with stories of its own.

THE MACKINAC BRIDGE

Good enough and excellent
are not nearly the same,
though some never bother
to learn the difference.

Good enough is a car ferry,
but you can't cross during storms
or when ice clogs the Straits,
and you'll wait days during hunting season.

Excellent is the world's
most beautiful suspension bridge,
five miles long and five lanes wide.
In bridges, in life, in love.

PAGAN BLESSINGS
Grand Rapids, Michigan 1965

My grandmother seldom spoke ill of others
though she disapproved of a local preacher
who wore a beret, drove a convertible,
and blessed his flock by invoking nature—
streams, butterflies, and sunshine—
but never Jesus Christ.

She simmered but did not boil over,
being a practical business owner
with family, friends, and clients
who took comfort in blessings dispensed
from that popular pagan pulpit
on Fountain Street, downtown.

ARKANSAS

1.
On a journey to Piggott,
where Hemingway and Pauline Pfeiffer
retreated to recover
from the recklessness of Paris,

I stop to contemplate the Mississippi
in Grand Tower and Cape Girardeau
watching barges move sand and stone
up and down its vast expanse

river of the Chickasaw and Sioux
river of Jim and Huckleberry Finn
river of Abraham Lincoln's journey
river of Langston Hughes' soul.

2.
I stop for lunch at a diner
where except for three state troopers
with disciplined brush-cuts
I am the only man without
a mesh cap promoting seed corn
or his favorite tractor,
the only man not dressed for the field,
the only man without a toothpick.

3.
The waitress at Sonic
is sixteen and full of life
and laughs when I ask
if I can leave a tip

and if I were her age
I would eat cheeseburgers
and drink chocolate shakes
all summer long.

I would tip her when I could,
and try to capture her joy
like a firefly in a jar
on a soft summer night.

4.
I met a woman in Kennett, Missouri—
beautiful and powerful with blue-black skin—
who told me there are towns nearby
where Black folk are not welcome.

We teach our children to stay away, she said,
and I allowed myself to believe
the place I come from is superior
until I traveled back home and read
of a Black man beaten senseless
in a small town up north.

5.
It is too early for horses
to be on pasture across the way,
though roosters compete
to challenge the sunrise.
Ninety degrees and one hundred by noon,
the last gasp of summer, my son says,
like a March snowstorm back home.

Birds I know call out —
crows, a cardinal, sparrows —
and then a mockingbird sings,
its song never heard
a long day's drive from here.

Inside the house a mother
makes breakfast and packs lunches,
all the while prodding and cajoling,
despairing homework undone
though oaths denying homework
were sworn the night before.

Across the street
a girl in a summer dress
positions the sprinkler for her father
before riding a skateboard
back down the driveway
and climbing into a black pick-up
for a ride to school.

And then an astonishing sight —
two Siberian Huskies
pull a bearded man on a skateboard
around this neighborhood of new homes —
war horses pulling a chariot
through the streets of ancient Rome.

And so are we reminded
to be grateful for blessings
both mundane and magnificent
at the dawn of each new day.

Amen.

6.
A billboard along Interstate 40
encourages drivers to Apply the Rod,
Save Your Child's Life!
though I'm quite sure Jesus,
who said suffer the little children
and spoke of millstones,
would not be happy if those children
came unto Him beaten and bruised.

Gettysburg

1.
CEMETERY RIDGE
September 2021

Birds sang on Cemetery Ridge today,
birds sang and a field of wheat
waved in the wind.

Did birds sing on that day?
Does wheat wave when God
looks the other way?

Union boys muttered and gasped
to see endless ranks of gray
form across the fields.

Rattling battle drums
could barely be heard
over silent Confederate prayers.

Artillery boomed, bayonets were fixed,
muskets roared, horses screamed,
dead men on the ridge, dead men in the field.

When did the birds sing again?
When did the wheat
wave again in the wind?

2.
THE SPIRITS GATHER

Set yersef down, Yank. Chaw?

> Nossir, never did acquire the taste.

Where was you fightin', friend?

> Behind the stone wall, at the angle. You?

Why, we was practically neighbors.
I was just the other side a' that copse of trees.

> Well friend, we was in the worst of it.

Yessir, that's a fact. How'd you meet your'n?

> Bayonet to the belly,
> courtesy 'a Armistead's boys.
> You?

Took grapeshot in my leg but tied it off
and kept chargin' 'til some poor fella
shot me dead from five foot 'er so.
Can't blame him none,
I'da kilt him next.

> Did he make it home?

No he never, dead just after me.
Met him here once. Nice fella,
hailed from 'round these parts.
His wife had a rough go of it
when he didn't come home.

        Lot of 'em did, wives and sweethearts.
         Think we'll move on from here, Reb?

Hope to, sure,
but a hunnert and fifty-some years
don't seem no more'n a couple 'a weeks.
What's yer plan, Yank?

        Likely same as you 'n ever'un else.
        I'll set here 'til it makes some sense.

Reckon we'll be here a while, friend.

        That's a fact, friend. That's a fact.

The spirits sit in silence until dawn,
content in each other's company.

3.
ON CONSECRATED GROUND

the spirits of two armies
gather where they died
on consecrated ground
at the peach orchard
the angle
the copse of trees
where the fields between ridges
were choked with dead
fathers sons grandsons
husbands nephews lovers
and the spirits cannot leave
though they were once sure
this place would crown them in glory
forever and ever hallelujah amen

Joseph Neely

I WOULD LIVE IN WALES

I would live in Wales
where poetry is written
by grandmothers and gardeners

for in America poetry is rare
beyond a responsible age
and absent the required degree

and here we whisper of poetry,
sharing our work only
with those we trust

so I would live in Wales,
where poetry is written
by bankers and butchers.

I would live in Wales,
where poetry is sometimes shouted
from the factory floor.

VENICE

We are reborn
several times each day,
crossing minor canals
and following sidewalks
too narrow for sunlight
to reach our feet.

Suddenly and without warning
we are thrust into brightness,
a piazza with cafés where couples
hold hands and drink wine,
serenaded by sparrows perched
on bare branches of stunted trees

and from our guidebook we learn
a Medici was executed here,
his death witnessed
by paving stones and statues
grown old long before
his final day

in this place where the works
of Renaissance masters
might be found behind any door,
decoration as common
as a stained-glass window
in a simple church back home.

POETS START EARLY

The neighbor walking her dog
has reason to believe she is the first
to take in this soft summer morning
but I've been watching for an hour
and she missed the sunrise,
a freight train whistle, a young buck,
two does and three spotted fawns,
hummingbirds and nuthatches,
squirrels playing tag in the grass,
three or four rabbits feasting on clover
and a whole hillside of chipmunks.

A POET'S DUTIES

1.
OF GIANTS AND SMALL GODS

On the day my friend
told me he had cancer
he also spoke of the day—
nearly 60 years ago—
when our 6th grade teacher
took him to a father-son dinner.

"My dad was dead and I was sure
that Cub Scout dinner
would be one more thing I missed
until my mom called out
'Your ride is here!'
and another voice—
I recognized it right away—
shouted 'Hurry up, we're late!'
so I flew down the stairs
and was the envy of every boy
at the dinner that night;
I've never forgotten that."

And so was I reminded
a poet must sing of giants
and praise small gods.

2.
JOHN KENYON

Every so often—
on the street or in a dream—
I run into someone who looks
like John might have looked
had he lived to finish college
and dress in the pin-stripe suit
I saw him wearing last week.

And so this, too, is a poet's job—
to remember and remind.

3.
ONE NEVER FORGETS

An old friend called today
to reveal that fifty years ago
he was abused by the doctor
our school system hired
to perform physical examinations
before the football season began,
examinations intended to protect
each child's health and safety.

I told him I loved him
and would help in any way I could,
then insisted he call a lawyer
instead of a poet.

A POEM LIKE A LIFE

A poem, like a life,
is never finished
and then one day it is.

The poet makes choices
adds or deletes
a word comma period
moves or discards
entire stanzas and
is forced to admit
the poem is not
remotely connected to
the sad joyful insight
which inspired
the first promising line
so many months ago
and when the poem at last
reads as it should
it is released
and cannot be recalled.

Only then does the poet
see the better path,
the way it could have been
from the very start.

Joseph Neely

THE POWER OF STORY

In the lower basilica of Assisi
a fresco shows Jesus on the cross
near two thieves
and I asked my wife—
fallen away now from her Catholic past—
if she knew why one thief wore a halo,
while the other hid his face.

Because the thief with the halo believed,
she replied, and Jesus told him
tonight you will be with me in Heaven
and we found ourselves unable to speak,
struggling to hold back our tears.

REASONS I GO TO CHURCH

Because my son's soccer team
never painted houses for the poor
over Spring Break in Mexico,
or raked leaves for old ladies
on the other side of town,
but his Sunday School class did.

Because folks from church
brought soup and casseroles
when I came home from the hospital,
but I never heard a word
from my friends at the bar.

Because a granddaughter asked,
the day after her sister died,
if I thought her sister
had already met Jesus
and I was never so certain
of anything in my life.

Joseph Neely

LEARNING OF GRACE

When I was a boy and very sick
my father sat by my hospital bed
and fed me treats from home,
but instead of being grateful
I complained he smelled of cigarettes
and uttered not a word of thanks.
He spoke to me gently,
washed his hands with lemon juice
and fed me more.

No sermon could convey
that lesson half so well,
for I did not deserve his kindness
and am sure I was never so gracious
towards a child of my own.

EVERY EASTER

Easter service is over
and my ears ring Hallelujah
as the congregation is released
to a bright spring morning,
but there are joggers in the street
and ads for Tiger baseball on the radio.
One neighbor mows his lawn
while another paints a shutter
and no one seems to understand
that everything has changed

and I am dismayed until I realize
it was probably like this
in Jerusalem, too,
that first Easter Sunday,
the whole town grateful
for a return to normal
after all the commotion
over two common thieves
and that noisy preacher,
the one from Nazareth.

RENDER UNTO CAESAR

A man at the gym wears a t-shirt
glorifying America's military might
and Christ's sacrifice on Calvary.

I stand for the flag,
his shirt proclaims, but also kneel
at the foot of the cross

and I wonder if he understands
that Jesus does not celebrate
the 4th of July.

ON A PROPOSAL
TO CHANGE THE NAME
OF ROBERT E LEE HIGH SCHOOL

A man on the radio
said he wouldn't mind
if his local high school
were named for Adolph Hitler
if that school also
had the best football team
in the whole damn state
and I was dumbfounded
when he was not struck dead
right there on the spot
but a few days later
the school's name was changed
so perhaps there is a God
and God simply works
in gentler ways.

Joseph Neely

TO SUCH AS THESE

A granddaughter told me,
when she was six or seven,
she saw God when she was born,
and that God has brown skin.

I believed her, of course,
but now she is ten and insists
she never said such a thing,
that she did not see God
and does not know
the color of God's skin.

But I have come to believe we all see God
at the instant we first draw breath,
and that God's skin is always
the color we each need it to be.

HEAVEN

My mother was certain
of harps and streets of gold,
and said she would straight away
make an egg salad sandwich
for her father, the gentle poet,
and apologize to her mother
because at last she understood,
understood, well . . . everything.
Her favorite dogs will be waiting—
C. S. Lewis said so—
to walk the beach and chase a stick.
Oh joyous, happy day!

Now grown cynical with age,
I fear Heaven may be no more
than accepting our imperfections
and being forgiven our foolishness
before becoming some small part
of what was and what will be.
Oh grey, nearly ordinary day.

If my mother's vision prevails
we'll share a summer-ripe tomato
from on top a shoreline dune
along Heaven's Lake Michigan,
watching August waves and waiting
for everyone we ever loved to join us.

Our dogs will lie easy in the sand—
Dewey, Piper, Rufus, Bear—
and take turns with the obligatory woof
should someone stroll past our perch.

THE HOLY PLAY DATE

The fresco depicts two babies—
John and Jesus—
playing at Mary's feet.
Their mothers were kin,
and John leapt in Elizabeth's womb
when Mary With Child came to call.

The Gospels give no guidance
but it makes sense the families
would want to celebrate
after the boys were born,
before Herod's soldiers fanned out
or perhaps even after the exile,
when Zechariah and Elizabeth
would have been older still,
but families will gather
despite age and illness
when any reunion might be the last.

John sheds no light,
insisting he didn't know Jesus
until the dove descended
and later sending a messenger
to ask, "Are you the one?"

forgetting, it seems,
his certainty on the Jordan
just a few years before.

So the holy play date
remains a mystery,
but mysteries of faith
are not the same as
a lack of faith AMEN.

A GIRL WITH NO NAME

This is what we know—
her father was a bigshot,
she was 12 years old,
and Jesus brought her back to life.
Today she might have braces,
wear a Red Wings jersey
and hang boy band posters
on pink bedroom walls.

"Don't tell anyone," Jesus asked,
but Peter, James and John,
the crowd, the pipe players,
kids climbing courtyard walls—
they knew.
Death was more public then,
and they laughed at Jesus
to think she might live again.
But he took her hand,

called to her spirit,
and commanded she be fed.

Was she celebrated or scorned,
a year later and the excitement gone?

Did neighbors call out to her
in the town's dusty streets,
or scurry quickly away?

Did childhood friends stay close?
Did she marry and have children,
or was she feared and shunned?

We supply our own ending,
and dare to hope one day
we might ask her ourselves.

JESUS LOVES THE LITTLE CHILDREN

You came with me to church
but had not yet absorbed
Christ's lessons of sacrifice
and placing a neighbor's needs
above your own
and so I admonished you,
at the Advent Dinner,
not to eat the Christmas cookies
before the meal was served—
cookies placed lovingly at each table
by church ladies who adored you—
and you agreed but took a bite
from each cookie decorated
in green frosting and sprinkles,
returning them to the communal plate
where they rested among lesser companions
your dental imprint in stark relief.

What are you doing? I asked in horror.
Those are my favorites, you explained,
and I want to be sure no one else eats them.

A PLEA TO CHILDREN NOW GROWN

I have dwelt among mermaids
and blasted through mountains
with dynamite and a pick.

I stood toe-to-toe
with the toughest man in the bar
and wrestled bears from a one-wagon circus.

I advised presidents,
positioned armies,
and built empires.

I bounced your babies
on my brittle knees
and they howled in delight.

I buried my parents—
as you will do soon—
and now I'm burying friends

so don't roll your eyes
at my suggestions
or dismiss me with a smile

for I have swum with mermaids
and gone three rounds
with a flea-bitten bear.

A GRANDMOTHER'S WISDOM

my grandmother told me
that money doesn't last
and I won't remember
raucous gin-soaked nights
but only quiet times
at home with those I love

embracing now the final quarter
how could I have questioned
a grandmother's wisdom

MY FATHER-IN-LAW

My father-in-law said "Oh yes!"
when I asked if he really ate
sausage made from pig ears and liver—
breakfast sausage called gritta—
while growing up in Fort Wayne,
and when he longed for one last taste
we followed a recipe written
in his daughter's hand
but dictated by his mother
on paper now stained and brittle.

Sharp bits of ear cartilage
convinced me this tradition
was well-served by death,
but my father-in-law was delighted
and filled empty margarine tubs
for his sister and brother,
certain that they, too,
would enjoy this final visit
with their ancestors in Fort Wayne.

THE ANCIENT *VOYAGEURS*

Chuck fixes my typewriters
but more importantly
called me badass
despite the fact I have
a sore back, too much belly
and brittle knees.

Chuck called me badass
after learning my brother and I
canoed a long river
though we were already old,
my brother more ancient and so
a bigger badass than I.

And now I'm grateful to Chuck
and think of him fondly,
for there is nothing more flattering
to an aging American man
than to be mistaken for badass
years after he last kicked ass.

Joseph Neely

Stripes and Plaids

It is not a pretty sight
when old men are left alone

with no one to remind them
to trim their eyebrows

that white pants should not be worn
with the first snow in the air

and that one must always assume
stripes and plaids will clash.

He dressed himself today
the country club ladies say

when lonely old men
wander in for dinner

but their husbands
barely glance up

for some things are not important
until the day they are.

FACING REALITY

There is an urgency
to mowing the lawn
with the sun going down
in late-September,
an urgency absent
in indolent, endless August

and beyond fair October
lurks grey November,
and while we expect
to be among the fortunate—
to emerge renewed in spring—
we put our affairs in order
should this be the year
our good fortune ends.

AT COSTCO

We walked past the food court
and towards the exit
when I turned at a tap on my hip
and struggled with a face I knew
from the school where I work.

"Hi, Mr. Joe," a child said,
and then I knew June,
her smile more radiant
than all the industrial lighting
in the ceiling above our heads.
"I'm with my parents," she explained,
as if I might not understand
nine-year-olds don't shop alone
on Friday night at Costco.

She hugged me without warning
and skipped back to the table
where her parents ate pizza,
and I smiled because ordinary outings
can lead to wondrous adventures
for young children and old men.

SENIOR MOMENTS

1.
we laugh when neither of us
can pull the word from our brain
and a few minutes later
when I shout "pickleball!"
it's funny as hell
until I'm alone at night
and looking over my shoulder
for more signs of the thief

2.
Little things like losing keys,
keys we have lost
since learning to drive,
raise the fear we'll soon
need help in all our tasks,
a tenacious weed with roots
which cannot be cleanly pulled.

Today we find
nearly everything lost
and can pretend the reckoning
is far off in the future,
but in quiet moments we know
the dot on the horizon
is around the next corner, too.

WHEN OLD MEN

1.
when old men nap
and then have trouble
returning to the here-and-now
it could be they are touring
'round the other side
and see some things
that look quite nice
but not yet so nice
they are ready to stay

2.
when old men cry
it is not in fear of death
but rather to pay
stinging-eyed tribute
to all they once loved
and all that once caused pain
their tears a final visit
with people and places
once near but now forever gone.

SMALL DREAMS

In the video French mourners
wear dark and dignified clothing
to Johnny Hallyday's funeral
and I decide to buy a grey suit
at the Black Friday sales,
my rumpled sport coat unworthy
even of French disdain.

And now I'm waiting
for someone I know to die
so that after the funeral
wives will turn to their husbands
and enthuse over the tailored fit
and the undeniable elegance
of my new grey suit.

RETIREMENT PLANS

The old man sits alone
as twilight turns dark
and dogs call to friends
off in the distance

while the radio at his feet
murmurs of Detroit Tigers who—
in the days of Kaline, Horton and Cash—
would be playing for Toledo

and from a chair
just inside his open garage
he waves but rarely speaks
to the few who pass by,

neighbors who wave in return
but also do not speak,
baseball, crickets and sprinklers
noise enough in the night.

INSTRUCTIONS UPON MY DEATH

I have seen obituary photos
chosen to settle a score,
so please find a photo
that suggests any pain I caused
has been forgiven.

No baseball hats or bellbottoms—
I survived beyond those things—
and no swilling Swedish vodka,
for I'll either die sober
or wishing that I had.

Wear happy clothes to my funeral.
Share a few poems and songs
then send me off to Amazing Grace,
for as often as I was lost
I was just as often found.

Speak of my best days and laugh,
then live a life crammed full
of kindness and fun stories
to share when we meet again
a bit further down the road.

SLOW RIVERS

I like to watch slow rivers
twist and bend downstream,
in no hurry to make their way
from one place to the next.

I admire mountain rivers, too,
rushing through gorges and over boulders,
intent on completing their journey
as quickly as they can.

My life is mostly slow rivers now—
deliberate, little rushing or bounding—
and I've learned all rivers set you down
at the same spot in the end.

A YARD LIKE A LIFE

When beginning a project
outside in the yard
my mind fills with tasks
not yet begun, and I pray
to one day be grateful
for all I've accomplished
and not filled with regret
at what remains undone.

Acknowledgements

My wife, Linda, encouraged me at every step in this project. The love poems in this book are for her. Our grandchildren are a constant source of inspiration and you'll find their stories here. The Eldons hung my poems on their refrigerator, like a drawing brought home from kindergarten.

Some of these poems first appeared on my blog, and I am grateful to friends, family and strangers who encouraged me in that effort.

Janice Warner produced original artwork for the front and back covers of this book. Trina Hayes and Lydia Cheatham provided valuable editing assistance. Jennifer Cook at Value Copy in Ann Arbor has been helping me for years; her patience knows no bounds.

My grandfather, Leonard Verschoor, was a gentle poet who wrote often of Lake Michigan. My mother, Catherine Verschoor Neely McNabb, was a fine writer who also loved the Big Lake. I am grateful the apple does not fall far from the tree.

God Bless us all, my family and yours.

Joseph Neely lives near Ann Arbor, Michigan with his wife, Linda, and a small white dog named Lincoln. Much of his life has been spent along the shores of Lake Michigan and he returns there often for inspiration. He got sober in 2012; these poems could not otherwise have been written. Help is available.